Boo

Reunited

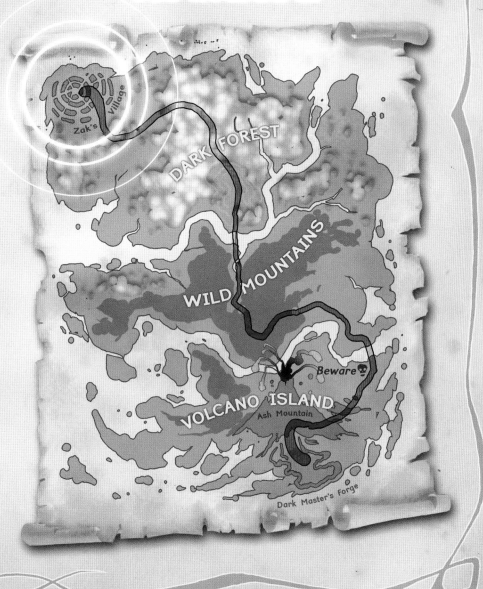

Zak's Village

DARK FOREST

WILD MOUNTAINS

Beware 💀

VOLCANO ISLAND

Ash Mountain

Dark Master's Forge

Reading Practice

u-e	ue	ew
use	cue	new
tube	due	few
cute	rescue	knew
fuse	argue	stew
mule	venue	view
abuse		nephew
refuse		curfew
accuse		

u

music

stupid

funeral

cucumber

Cuba

student

At the bottom of each page of text, some multisyllable words are split up for the reader.

Contents

Vocabulary:

mused	–	gazed thoughtfully
weary	–	tired
resume	–	to start again after stopping
futile	–	pointless
assume	–	to suppose
consumed	–	ate or drank
spurred	–	urged the mule to walk on (as if with spurs)
fuming	–	very angry
mint	–	to make coins or medals by stamping metal
unite	–	to join together

Chapter 1
"You Must Resume the Quest!"

Zak lay restless in his bed. He could not sleep. "Tomorrow, I will be fourteen. I wonder what the next year will bring?" he mused about his future. He felt weary, but his body refused to sleep.

fu ture   re fused

Suddenly, the old woman appeared to Zak. He knew he was not dreaming.
"Zak!" she called out to him.
"You must resume the quest!"

"Why?" Zak asked.
"The Dark Master is furious!" she continued.
"He is making a brand new talisman for himself. It will be truly powerful! We must unite to fight him!" she said.

re sume   fu ri ous   u nite

"He will mint the new talisman from metal. You must travel to Volcano Island and stop him. The Dark Master will be able to change into any evil being. Humankind is at risk."

Vol ca no   Hu man kind

Chapter 2
Useless Junk

The next day, Zak told Grandpa about the old lady. "You must save mankind!" Grandpa said. "I refuse to go," Zak cried. "You must!" Grandpa said, sadly.

"This is a futile quest!" Zak cried. "How can I defeat the Dark Master with this? The talisman is all used up!" He hurled the talisman at the wall. It shattered and fell to the floor in pieces.

re fuse   fu tile   shatt ered

"What have you done?" Grandpa cried out in horror. "Now there is no hope at all!" Zak was furious with himself. He sank to his knees in despair. Then, a few of the broken pieces began to glow. They fused into a new talisman.

fu ri ous   des pair

Zak showed Mim the new talisman.

"I assume I will be coming?" she asked.

"It would be useful if you stayed to protect Grandpa from the Dark Master," Zak said. Mim did not argue.

"This is a map of Volcano Island," said Grandpa. "There are a few old yew trees here. Use them if you need shelter."

a ssume   use ful   ar gue

Chapter 3
The Mule

When Grandpa got back from market, he had a mule walking behind him. It looked starved and abused. Mim scrubbed him down and gave him some food. The mule consumed it hungrily.

a bused   con sumed

Chapter 4
Zak Sets Off

The next day, Zak set off. Grandpa had packed the mule with food and fuel. "Wish us good luck!" Grandpa wept. He watched Zak until he was out of view.

Zak stopped to rest under the old yew trees. The new talisman hung heavily around his neck. He took it off and hung it on a branch.

fu el   hea vi ly

Zak used sticks for fuel. He sat by the fire and fell asleep. When he woke up the next morning, the talisman had gone! Zak began to panic. How could he have been so careless and stupid?

care less   stu pid

Chapter 5
Mim to the Rescue!

The quest was over! He might as well go back to the village. The mule refused to move. Zak jumped onto the mule and spurred him on. "Stupid beast!" he hissed. The mule bucked and Zak flew off, crash, right into a trap.

Zak looked up from the pit, helpless and fuming. "Is this what you are looking for?" Zak saw a hand dangling the talisman above his head.

vill age   stu pid

"Shall I rescue you?" said Mim, as she dropped the talisman into his hand. Quick as a flash, Zak turned into a lynx. The lynx leapt out of the trap in one jump. The mule looked on, very confused.

res cue   con fused

"Admit it!" Mim teased. "You had to be rescued from that pit!"

"Did you leave Grandpa on his own?" Zak asked. "He insisted," said Mim.

"He said I would be more useful here with you!" Zak knew that Grandpa was right.

res cued   in sist ed